The Voiceless Child

7 Keys To Discovering Your Purpose And Unlocking Your Destiny

By Sherry Donahue-Brown

Copyright © 2016 by Sherry Donahue-Brown

All rights reserved. This book or any portion thereof may not be reproduced or used in any manner whatsoever without the express written permission of the publisher except for the use of brief quotations in a book review.

Printed in the United States of America

First Printing, 2016

ISBN-13: 978-1535104371
ISBN-10: 1535104376

Dedication

I would like to dedicate this book to God who allowed me to go through the fire many times only to come out NOT smelling smoky.

I would like to dedicate this book to my spouse, Stafford E Brown, Sr. whose unwavering commitment to marriage and family opened my heart and taught me to love. The one who encouraged, inspired, and supported me through this process and many others.

To my children whose existence gave me the strength to persevere through the many storms that we were faced with.

To the Pool/Vernon family who allowed God to open their hearts, home, and minds to choose me and introduced me to a better way of life.

To my siblings; Pamela, Casey, Gregg, and Michael for your ongoing support.

To the Branch/Breed family for inviting my children and I into your lives and showering us with unconditional love and acceptance.

To my family & friends who didn't allow me to give up or stop seeing the vision.

To my church family, Quinn's Chapel AME, where it all started with the foundation of my spiritual life through teachings and memorizing scriptures. I didn't realize that those scriptures memorized as a child would help me in my adult life.

Table of Contents

Chapter 1 - The Beginning of Voicelessness 7

Chapter 2 – The Awakening 19

Chapter 3 - The Compass 27

Chapter 4 - What's the Purpose of Your Purpose 35

Chapter 5 - Direction of Your Destiny 45

Chapter 6 - Obvious Obstacles or Overcoming Opportunities 53

Chapter 7 - The Seven Keys to Discovering Your Purpose and Unlocking Your Destiny 59

Chapter 8 - Newness: Learning to Take Destiny Steps ... 69

Chapter 9 - Press Towards Your Purpose Through Your Pain 77

Chapter 10 - Can You Hear Me Now? I'm a Purpose Walker! 83

Main Principles 90

Quotes 92

Chapter 1 - The Beginning of Voicelessness

Voicelessness – silent; mute; having no voice in the management or control of affairs; uttering no words; unspoken; no vote or having no choice.

Main Principle

Although situations and circumstances can take your voice away and cause you to become silent and mute, it doesn't have to be permanent. Your voice can be heard. #TheVoicelessChild

As long as I can remember I called myself a loner; the little girl who often desired to be by herself. I lacked confidence and had low self-esteem. Many times I questioned, "Why?" asking myself, "Where did it come from?"

As I reflected on my life, I was reminded of the horrible day in November of 1974. I was a five-year-old child who had never been to school. I couldn't read or even write my name. I remember as I played outside in the dirt making mud pies, I heard a noise from a vehicle. I looked up to see a long, brownish driving up and parking in front of my granny's window. I found out later it was a station wagon from Child Services. In the vehicle was a tall, white man wearing dark slacks with a white shirt and tie. He was the passenger and an African American lady, wearing a tannish colored pant suit, was the driver.

The man walked over towards my sibling and me who were under the pavilion playing in the dirt. He picked me up, carried me by my belt loop as if I were a ragged doll, pinching only the low waist of my pants. While the man carried me, I heard a lady far off screaming loud, "NO, NO, NOOOOOOO, PLEASE NO! PUT HER DOWN!"

I was also screaming for someone, anyone to, "HELP ME!" but no one came. We arrived to the vehicle where he tossed me on to the backseat. I began beating on the windows, crying out loud, and I continued screaming. Still, no one came. I wondered where everyone was. Where was my family? Where were they going to take me?

I wasn't in a car seat or a seat belt so I kicked, screamed, and cried. Since no one came, I didn't think I was heard. The man and lady returned to the car, started it up, backed out, and drove off with me in it, screaming, crying, and kicking.

Our destination ride seemed like an eternity. It was somewhere far away in another town and parish. I didn't know where I was, why I was taken, or when I would return. Would someone come and get me? I quickly remembered that my family didn't have a car to come and get me.

I was taken to the Department of Health and Human Services or DHS. Upon my arrival there, I was placed in a room where people who worked there passed by, looking into the room at me as if something was wrong with me. On that dreadful day in November, while in the Department of Human Services office, my appearance was less than attractive. I was unkempt, dirty, and my hair had not been combed or washed in a long time. It was plaited up in twisted twigs and I wasn't even wearing shoes. I didn't remember the last time I had a bath, wore shoes, or had my hair combed.

Finally, the same lady who drove the car earlier when they had taken me from my home brought some adults into the room. At that time, different strangers came in and looked over me and chose someone else. I felt as if I was in a meat market with strangers looking and picking over me. Finally, someone selected me and I had a place to go. As a child, I was in a strange place, with strange people, didn't know what was happening, what they would do with me, or what they would do to me. The man and lady who took me finally came and said, "You are going to a new home," without an explanation of "WHY!" At that time, I became a "Ward of the State."

What is a ward of the state? The ward of state means the legal responsibility of your biological parents has been temporally removed concerning you. The state removes children from their natural environments, placing them with a foster family.

A foster family is a family assigned by a Social Worker to provide care (total care) for a child or children when the state removes you from your biological family, when no relatives are available to provide care for you. The Social Worker is in place to act as an advocate for you, the child. If a child is not happy with/in their current placement, the social worker is in place to assist with getting things worked out.

It appears that as a child in Foster Care, your voice and opinion don't really count. In addition, the Social Worker becomes your surrogate parent and everything you would like to do goes through them. The Social Worker (State) makes the final decision. For example, I wanted to go out for cheerleading and I did, however, it was with restrictions. I made the cheerleading squad but when the final word came in from the state, I couldn't go to away games so I had to leave the squad.

As a child, it was very frustrating because I had to be someone perfect because whatever the state said was gospel. I simply had to be alright with the State's decision in an effort not to leave my placement. If you, as a child, challenged the State's decision, they could choose to remove you from your placement or there could be other consequences. Therefore, you learned quickly to be an obedient/pleaser. That was the beginning of my voicelessness. That was when fear and rejection began in my life.

Rejection

Rejection is the act or process of rejecting or the state of being rejected; refusing to believe, accept, or consider.

We all have a fundamental need to belong and rejection destabilizes that need. When we get rejected, our need to belong becomes destabilized and the disconnection we feel adds to our emotional pain. Feeling alone and disconnected after rejection has an impact on our behavior.

Rejection puts us in a place of fear. This fear is based on not losing what we have. We are afraid that at any moment the other shoe could drop and we will lose everything.

As a result of this intense fear, my emotions were all over the place and it caused me to be numb. It was easier not to feel anything so I learned to cope. I learned to cope by perfecting everything that I did. I became a "Miss Goody Two-Shoes," a true people pleaser. I never wanted to cause a ruckus. I felt that in order to maintain any sense of stability in my life, I needed to become and remain compliant.

Rejection seeks and destroys our self-esteem by causing us to find faults in ourselves, focusing on our inadequacies, and kicking ourselves when we're already down. Blaming yourself attacks your self-worth and deepens the emotional pain you feel.

Rejection does not respond to reason. Your ability to reason with others lessens because others do and have done little to soothe your hurt feelings. In addition, rejection creates anger and aggression in you. Also, as you recall experiences of rejection, you relive either the emotional or physical pain of rejection.

Adjustments

The first thing I remember when I arrived at the new home was getting a bath in a tub. I was horrified because bathing was not my norm. I began to get my hair combed, which was painful. As a five-year-old, I was faced with adult decisions including a new family and at school. On my first day of school, I was terrified because I had to adjust. A newbie who lacked confidence, communication, and social skills quickly learned to listen and observe others while fitting in a school setting. I didn't know what to say to others because I didn't have any friends and lacked the skills to make friends appropriately. I had to learn to think before speaking.

Even though I had a new home, family, and a new school making friends, I wasn't sure if I could trust any of them or how long I would be at either location. So I felt like I was by myself most of the time. As time progressed and I grew older, I was able to stay in my original placement. I was truly thankful for that because many times children go from home to home placements and I did not. Being in one placement, I received acceptance, stability, positive guidance, and went to church. However, I felt I did not have a voice so I was essentially a VOICELESS CHILD.

> "Without a voice, I'm invisible."
> Sherry Donahue Brown
>

In my opinion a voiceless child is an individual who is unable to speak or express themselves freely and honestly to others. In others words, the voiceless child is a person lacking the power or right to express an opinion or exert control over affairs.

No Words

> *"Did vanishing words lead to the vanishing voice, or did the vanishing voice lead to the vanishing words?"*
> Sherry Donahue Brown
>
>

There came a time in my life where the words seemed to stop coming out of my mouth. We all have a need to be heard. When we ask a question, we expect someone to step up and answer. I became accustomed to just holding my tongue and not asking. There was a sense of loneliness and being alone although I had my foster family. I could be in a crowded room with 20 people and I still felt alone. I felt invisible.

Sometimes I would try to engage and be the center of attention and other times I would just go to my room. I often wondered if I fit in. I would envision my family and I would try to see where I fit. I always felt like a misfit, which caused me to feel invisible. Some of the things we experience in life continuously try to silence us. But as we move forward, we see that our voices aren't muted forever. There is hope.

Trying To Fit In

Are you a shopper? Well, I'm a shopper! Do you like trying on clothes? I hate trying on clothes, especially when I'm between sizes. What is between sizes? Between sizes is when you're not the size you used to be, and you're not the size you want to be. So you try on the size you used to be and it's too small. Then you try on the size you want to be and it's too big. It's like that when you are a foster child. You are not in the environment where you used to be and you trying to fit into the environment where you are. You don't know where you want to be and you can't return to where you use to be.

At the age of five, going to school for the first time, I had to adjust. I wasn't where I used to be, which was outside playing the dirt. I am now I'm in school, sitting with my peers as they look at me. So I ask myself the question, "What do I say? Will you be my friend? But what if they tell me no?" As I observe, these children have been together since August and now it's November. They are in groups and already have friends. They have pencils and are writing; they have crayons and are coloring. What do I do? I have never written or colored before. *Lord, please help me.*

I recall a few months after I started school, one of my classmates made it known to everyone he didn't want to be my friend. He did not play with me and refused to talk to me. My raw insecurities kicked into overdrive. I was five years old! I had no idea what I had done to this kid. So one day my class and I were returning to class from lunch, preparing to go on the playground and play. As we began to walk down the stairs, this kid pushed me down the stairs. I busted my head and knocked out four teeth. (Remember, I'm still in kindergarten trying to fit in.) I was rushed to the hospital and my foster parents came. Then the state stepped in to investigate.

After returning to school, we were separated from each other and weren't in the same class anymore. As I recall, this was the beginning of my school issues as I adjusted to my new environment. I was bullied, made fun of, teased, and called out of my name. As a child, all I wanted was a friend who I could trust and to belong.

Fitting in Family

My family was awesome! They welcomed me immediately! However, I remember being afraid and unsure of every single thing. The very first thing I did in my new environment (home) was to take a bath. This was unfamiliar to me because in my previous environment I didn't remember taking bathes. I literately had to learn to bathe in a tub. Then I got my hair washed and combed. Oh my gosh, what a painful experience this was. I was given the nickname "Weeble Wobble" because my head moved around so much. I had new, clean clothes to wear with new underwear.

As a child my first thought was, "Why are these strangers being nice to me?" Well, as time passed, the niceness continued. There were doctor appointments, hair appointments, church events, and more. Each day I wondered why and when was the nice treatment going to end. It didn't!

My Voice Unmuted

Unmuted is to restore the sound or output in something or someone which was previously muted. Restore is to give back, reinstate, to return something to an earlier or original condition back into existence or use.

How was my voice restored? In order for restoration to occur there are steps that must be taken. My steps were prayer, counseling, and forgiveness.

Prayer is the practice of a simple conversation with God. It doesn't have to be elaborate or special. It has to be sincere with making your desires and request known unto God, who is the creator of all and can do all. Prayer is admitting our needs, adopting humility, and claiming dependence upon God. So my simple request to God was, "HELP ME." This caused an internal dialogue which I believe created a deeper, stronger, more intimate relationship with God. I realized that even though man didn't understand me, my Daddy understood me. I felt like I may have been rejected by my biological parents but my heavenly Father never rejected me.

> *"Who can hear me? I need God to hear me."*
> Sherry Donahue Brown

Counseling is the provision of assistance and guidance in resolving personal, social, psychological problems, and difficulties that have happened in your life by a professional. How do you know that you are in need of counseling? I was told I needed counseling by my Social Worker because the event I experienced was traumatic and I developed temporary amnesia of my life prior to the date I was removed from what I had known for five years of my life as "HOME." Little did I know at that time, I would never return. As a result, my counselor was there to assist me in adjusting to my new home environment. In addition to my counselor helping me to adjust physically she also helped me emotionally to adjust. For the most part, you can forget it, but there is a part of that pain you remember. As you remember the pain, you become careful and cautious around people. You decide that you don't want to experience that pain again. When you are rejected from such a young age, it creates deep trust issues. This makes you suspicious and hard to trust people because you think they have an ulterior motive. You also think you are not good enough to befriend others. Therefore, your counselors teach you to accept yourself, set boundaries, and develop appropriate social and communication skills.

Forgiveness is the act or process of being forgiven; to give up resentment of or claim to something be given in return, compensation, or retaliation. Forgiveness does not mean forgetting nor does it mean condoning or excusing others for the offenses. Through forgiveness you can help repair a damaged relationship. It doesn't obligate you to reconcile with the person who harmed you or release them from legal accountability.

The first step to understanding forgiveness is learning what it is and isn't. Forgiveness is letting go of the need for revenge and releasing negative thoughts of bitterness and resentment. Once I gave my voicelessness to God to help me forgive those who hurt me and releasing the pain was actually the beginning of hearing myself. I was off mute (unmuted) and speaking to be heard, not boldly at first but speaking to be heard nevertheless. It didn't happen overnight. It was a long process. Forgiveness is an intentional and voluntary process by which a victim undergoes a change in feelings and attitude. When you forgive others - know that God is WILLING to give you a FRESH START!

Finally, as I abide and live fully in my relationship with Jesus Christ, I no longer have to live in the silence of my past. My voice can no longer be muted. The past can't mute it. Fear can't mute it. Rejection can't mute it. The system can't mute it. I can speak now, be heard, and be understood.

My Thoughts

In what areas of my life have I allowed my voice to be silenced?

My Biggest Takeaways and Action Items From This Chapter

Chapter 2 – The Awakening

Awaken – to stop sleeping: to wake up.

Main Principle
Just as your physical body needs rest so do your emotions; just as your physical body awakens, it's now time to awaken your emotions. #TheVoicelessChild

Are you a morning person? How long does it take for you to wake up in the morning?

For me, waking up is a process. When the alarm goes off, I hit the snooze button. I usually hit the snooze button three to five times. The snooze button acts as a warning, letting you get a few more minutes of sleep before it rings again. Finally, I'll get up and sit on the bed but I'm still half asleep. It is not until I begin to walk that I finally wake up.

Once I begin to walk, I become less sleepy and more energized. As I begin to move, my heart begins to pump faster and the blood begins to circulate through my body. As I move, my lungs begin to take in more air and the increase in oxygen begins to energize my body as well. By the time I take a few steps, I feel much more awake than I did sitting at the side of the bed. But, I couldn't just sit on the side of the bed and wait for the energy to come. The energy came as I started to move.

As I think about the process I go through to awaken my physical body, I realize I am going through a similar process with my emotions. Are my emotions completely awakened or are they sitting on the side of the bed?

Emotions Not Awakened

When I think about my emotions "sitting on the side of the bed," I think about how sometimes it's hard for me to feel. It's hard for me to express my emotions. It's hard for me to do certain things.

As with the physical, you can't wait for emotional energy to come before you express emotions. You have to express your emotions first and then continue to build on that emotional energy.

Do you allow yourself to feel happiness and joy? Do you allow yourself to become excited and thrilled about things or do you suppress your emotions? Do you know what you are passionate about?

If you're not fully awake emotionally, it's really hard to fully discover your purpose or identify your destiny. It's really hard because we walk into our purpose based on what we are passionate about and what we feel. "I really like this or I really like that!" If your emotions are not awakened, then you don't feel it. If you don't feel it, you don't like it and then you won't do it. It's similar to hitting the snooze button over and over before getting up.

Emotional Awakening

To be fully awake you must have a relationship with God. You have to allow God to teach you to forgive those who have hurt you.

When I was a young adult, one of the things that almost hardened me was an incident I recalled with my mother. My birth mother and I didn't have a relationship. I recall once when we had a disagreement and she really expressed herself. She told me that she didn't want me and that she never wanted me. To think that I went from being rejected by my birth mother to now knowing that I wasn't wanted was more hurtful.

So I asked her, "Why didn't you just abort me?"

She told me, "I tried to kill you but you wouldn't die."

It was 1 year later that she died.

It took God for me to identify the feelings of anger, bitterness, and resentment I had inside. I had to decide to turn those feelings into forgiveness. I truly had to forgive her. The hard part was she was no longer here. The damage she had done had piled up over the years and not until I said, "I forgive her," that I began to feel and to wake up emotionally.

Who Woke You Up?

I think it had to be God that woke me up. As we forgive and lean not unto our own understanding, we experience this process of awakening. God woke me up. He would not allow me to sleep my life away emotionally.

I trust in God. God gives the ability to trust man. If God doesn't put it in you, you will think everyone is going to reject you. You look for acceptance and as you forgive others, you will accept others. God gives you the ability to forgive those who hurt you. We tend to lean to the past but God will lead us into the future.

Accept God's Word for what it is. Forgive others as God has forgiven us. There is an old saying, "When you know better, you do better." We have to look at people in their environment and their context. When I think of my mother, I wonder did she really know better? What did she know? Did she know that drinking was going to lead to her death? Did she know that drinking was going to lead to her losing all of her children? If she knew this, would she have continued to drink?

Since drinking did, in fact, lead to her death, I will never get the answer. I had to step back and give it to God. I said, "God, I don't know what to do with this and I release it to You." When you do this, you are releasing the pain and the unknown. You are releasing the things you don't have control over and those things that have caused you pain. You realize it wasn't your fault.

There are times I have to say to myself, "Sherry, it was not your fault." I have to realize that I am not the victim. I have the victory. I am still here. As I reflect on my biological mother, I realize that she was a victim and that victim mentality led to her death.

As I wake up and as I awaken, I still have the opportunity to operate in my purpose and in my destiny.

It's Okay To Feel

When we talk about awakening to your emotions, we are not just talking about those emotions that we deem as "good" such as happiness and joy. We are also talking about awakening to emotions such as sadness and anger. Many times we will keep our emotions bottled up on the inside and we don't let people know how we feel. We must be able to let people know when they have hurt us or when they are doing things concerning us that we do not feel are appropriate.

> "Emotions make you cry sometimes."
> Sherry Donahue Brown

Emotions make you cry sometimes and that is okay. Sometimes our emotions are all over the place. Sometimes I don't know if I'm going, coming, sitting, or standing. Sometimes you cry for no reason. It's okay to cry. Crying is a symbol of releasing the pain, bitterness, resentment, guilt, and shame. We also have to release that root of rejection or it's going to prevent us from reaching our fullest potential.

Walking to Your Purpose and Destiny

As a mother, I didn't think I was good enough for my children. I did not think that I deserved to have my children. I was parenting, not knowing and going through the motions, just wanting to be a better parent. I didn't have a really good example of a parent. I had challenges with parenting that helped me to get educated. I strived to do things differently from what had happened to me.

One of my children had a stroke at three months old and was diagnosed with having a very rare disorder. My child is the only one in the U.S. and ten countries with this disability.

How does this tie into my purpose and my destiny? As a result of my child's disability, I have gained so much experience from parenting my children. I am able to be a blessing to others by sharing my experience. I have a business where I serve and mentor parents. If my child did not have this disability, I would not have this business. The awakening has helped me to walk in my purpose.

> "Get up, Get up, Get your emotions up."
> Sherry Donahue Brown
>

I would tell my children when they were young, "Get up, get up, get your butt up." This became a song for us. I would also say, "It's time, it's time, it's time to make that change," as they would prepare to go to school. I explained to them that they were changing from being at home to being at school.

You are transitioning from getting up to trying to make a change. When you put the two little songs together, it becomes, "It's time, it's time for us to get up. It's time for us to make that change." For many of us, it's time for us to truly get unstuck. It's time for us to be awakened. It's time for us to truly live on purpose. It is time to walk in our destiny.

We have gone from not having a voice, to being awakened and now to walking. Now it's time to activate the compass so that we are walking along the correct path.

> "*It's time, it's time to make that change.*"
> Sherry Donahue Brown
>

My Thoughts

Are there areas where I am not awakened to my emotions? Explain.

My Biggest Takeaways and Action Items From This Chapter

Chapter 3 - The Compass

Compass – an instrument used for finding direction

Main Principle
We must follow the direction that God is leading us as we would follow a compass. If we have made bad choices, it's not too late to get back on track.
#TheVoicelessChild

My Compass

Growing up I remember I wanted to be an attorney. I envisioned myself walking up and down the stairs in some of the most powerful court buildings in Washington D.C. I could see myself being a prosecutor. Wearing navy and black suits, with coordinating shirts and heels was my vision. This was the path I started on when I entered college. However, what choice did I make? I got pregnant in college.

After finishing my first degree, I wondered if I could go back to school. But instead of entering law school, I was entering motherhood. My compass had to change. It changed from law school to motherhood; from being a student to being a mother and from being a student to being an employee. My choice changed the direction of my life at that point. The decisions we make can absolutely alter and change the direction of our lives.

Compass vs. GPS

Most people are familiar with a compass. It is an instrument used for finding direction and it has been around for centuries. With the typical magnetic compass, the needle always points towards the north pole. If you are stranded somewhere and you can't determine which way north is, a compass will point you in the right direction.

A compass is great for finding directions but unless you know what direction your destination is in; it is of little use. You still need a map and you need to know where your destination is relative to where you are. If you are lost in the woods and you know there is a road south of the woods, you can use the compass to determine which way south is. However, if you have no idea which direction the road is, this information is of little value.

Fast forward to 1973, when work began on the Global Positioning System (GPS). This space-based navigation system, initially designed for military use, provided the missing pieces for true navigation. Not only was it able to point you in the direction desired (north, south east or west), it was also able to tell you where you were as well as give you directions to where you want to go, provided that you know where you want to go.

A GPS, which is now readily available on any smart phone, can give you turn by turn directions verbally. It will even try to reroute you if you miss a turn or direction. However, it is still up to you to make the turn and follow the directions. The choice is still yours.

I want you to think about yourself; think about where you wanted to go and where you are now. What choices have you made in life that hasve altered and changed the direction you were once headed?

I would visualize being an attorney. I could see myself with the home and the car and the outfits. I could even the see the accessories, down to the shoes and purses. But that was all in my head. My choices did not support the vision I maintained in my head at the time.

> "The difference between what lies behind us and what lies ahead of us is the choice that we make in the moment."
> Sherry Donahue-Brown
>

Instead of walking up the stairs to the Federal Courthouse, I was walking into a food stamp office because my income simply was not enough to support my family. Instead of learning tort law and legal definitions, I was learning how to ask for assistance at the welfare office. I had to learn the language; I had to learn to ask for different things. The distance between where I was and where I wanted to be was night and day. It was north and south.

I was not where I wanted to be but I could blame no one. It was my compass; it was my choice. This does not mean that I don't love my children. I cannot imagine my life without them. It was a choice and that choice changed my direction and life.

The Directions In My Life

I often refer to the different time periods of my life in reference to the directions on a compass. During those times where I was voiceless and making bad decisions in my life, I envisioned myself moving "down" or "south." When I made decisions that reflected more positive choices in my life, I considered that my "north" as I saw myself as moving upward. Movement that was neither positive nor negative I saw as going "east" or "west."

When I entered college, full of hope and determination of becoming an attorney, I was definitely heading north. I was moving up and I was overcoming some of the obstacles of my childhood. But I found that I had not completely dealt with some of those issues in my past. I was still plagued by the horrors of rejection and poor self-esteem. So when the first guy came along that said, "Oh, you're cute," I found myself making decisions that did not support the vision I had for my life. As a result, I ended up pregnant, alone, and heading in the southern direction of my life.

I didn't like where I was. I didn't like the unsteady employment, going into the WIC office, or being almost evicted from the apartment that I had just moved into. I had to change my direction. I did this mentally and physically.

Originally, I am from Louisiana. I literally packed up what I had and moved west to Texas. I still didn't have anything and I was still on state assistance but my eyes were opened and I was allowing my compass to lead me in a different direction. I said, "Lord, I don't know what all of this means, but you have a purpose for it in my life."

The Purpose

I didn't even know the meaning of the word "purpose" when I said this. However, this was the prayer that was on my heart. This was the word I used in my conversations with God. In that critical time of my life when I had nothing but my children and a couple of bags of clothes, taking public transportation, I felt God was moving me slowly in the direction He wanted me to go. Small, baby steps, I was slowly heading north in my life. I feel that if you're headed north, you are going in the right direction.

Never Alone

You run into many people while you are on this journey called life. Although you may feel that you are alone, you are never truly alone. You are surrounded by people, whether it is your family, co-workers, friends or a companion. You must be careful that the people who you share your journey with, those that will have the greatest impact and influence in your life, have your best interests in mind. You don't want someone to lead you in the wrong direction.

Likewise, you want to make sure that the people around you are vested in your success. For instance, in the military, you are given a buddy when you go out on assignments, even if it is just for training. You never go out alone. You always have someone with you. That is

> *"The difference between the impossibility and possibility is your determination."*
> Sherry Donahue-Brown
>

why you never see a soldier alone; you always see more than one. If one gets hurt, or is attacked, you have someone to fight with you and to be on alert or lookout where you can't see. But here is the interesting part; even when you test, you test as a team. If you fail, your team fails and you come back as a team and you retest as a team. Therefore, each person on the team is personally vested in your success. We have to be selective about who we select to be on our team.

Knowing Who You Are

Oftentimes we see ourselves in connection with the people we have on our team. When I was younger, I was searching for someone to validate me. I was also searching for an identity. But when you know who you are and whose you are, you are not searching for someone to validate you. You are comfortable in your own skin and you are free to move in the direction of your destiny and travel north.

As you find your voice and become awakened to the possibilities in your life, it's time for you to evaluate your direction. What direction are you going in? What choices are you making? What short term and long term effects will the choices you are making right now have on your future? We must follow the direction that God is leading us as we would follow a compass. If we have made bad choices, it's not too late to get back on track. We have all made choices that have had both positive and negative effects on our lives. For many of us, our journey has been all over the map: north, south, east and west. Just remember, you have the power to change direction at any time.

My Thoughts

Where do I want to go in my life? Where do I see myself 5 years from now?

_____

_____

_____

_____

_____

_____

_____

_____

_____

My Biggest Takeaways and Action Items From This Chapter

Chapter 4 - What's the Purpose of Your Purpose

Purpose – the reason for which something is done, created or for which something exists.

Main Principle
When God has you on an assignment, He provides the picture, the people, the places, and the pieces in an effort to bring His vision to past.
#TheVoicelessChild

To every thing there is a season, and a time to every purpose under the heaven:

Ecclesiastes 3:1

For I came down from heaven, not to do mine own will, but the will of him that sent me.

John 6:38

What is Purpose

Although there are tons of programs, seminars, conferences and books (including the one you are reading) which talk about purpose, the true definition of purpose is very simple. Purpose simply means the reason for which something is done, created, or for which something exists. It answers the question, "Why." Why am I doing this thing? Why was I created? Why am I here?

There is a purpose for everything that God created. God had a reason. Oftentimes, we struggle because we don't understand the reason. This was something that Jesus did not struggle with. He knew what his reason was for being here. Since he understood his purpose, he knew what to expect. He understood He was coming to give up His life to save a world that would not accept or appreciate Him. Therefore, He didn't second guess himself when rulers of the day didn't welcome Him with open arms. He didn't think, "What's wrong? Why aren't things going well?"

This is the question we often ask when things are not going well. We think that something has gone wrong if we are experiencing challenges in our lives. Many times there are some things that have gone astray. While that may be the reason that something has happened, it is not the purpose behind why it happened.

Life has taught me that there is a purpose in everything that happens. There is a purpose in the pain and in the struggle we are going through. That purpose may be to create

"A delay is not a denial."
Unknown

character, teach us patience, or to teach us something else. Many times, it is in the struggle that we find our purpose and we are able to identify the assignment God has for us.

Identify the Assignment

As a child, I wasn't very sensitive or compassionate. I didn't feel that I had a voice and I shutdown my feelings to the point that I felt numb. I felt emotionally disconnected. But then things happened in my life that helped me develop a sense of gratitude and compassion. Being a ward of the state and being on state assistance made me appreciate being in the position to not have to be on state assistance. Having a child with disabilities helped me to become sensitive and compassionate. This gave me a heart to work with children and adults with disabilities. I don't think I would be as attuned with the parents and the consumers if I did not have my own child.

A part of my purpose in life is to meet the families where they are, empathize with them, and to let them know that I'm right there with them. I recognize my value as a resource because I have experienced many of the things my consumers are experiencing and I have walked in their shoes. There are times when I am able to tell the families about certain doctors because I have taken my child to them. There are times when a family would call and say, "Mrs. Brown, I'm going through this," and I can empathize with them because I understand what they were going through.

I understand the pain and I am familiar with the struggle they face. When I first began this journey, I was alone. There was no one for me to call. No one really understood what I went through. Because of this, I can comfort others that face these same challenges.

Life Experiences

When my mother passed suddenly a few years ago, I suffered from tremendous grief. Her birthday and Mother's Day are around the same time. I was a behavioral educator at this time and I walked away. I didn't know what it meant or what it would lead to in the future. I was grief stricken for about 6 months.

During that time, I felt like I had no direction. But it was during that time that God gave me a vision. He named the vision. I remember being so excited. I said to my husband, "I know where I'm going to work and what I'm going to do. I told him what God told me.

Frantically I searched for the name on Google but I couldn't find it anywhere. So I said, "Ok Lord, where is it?"

God replied, "This is what you're going to do."

I said, "What are you talking about God? What do you mean; this is what I'm going to do?

I didn't hear any other explanation at the time. I had no idea what this was. Initially I thought that it had something to do with the local 911 police dispatch department. I figured that was something I could do but I didn't pursue it at that time.

Shortly after that, someone said to me, "You know Sherry, there is a need for providers in the county. You take such good care of your children. Whenever you see they, they are not wanting for anything. They are always clean and happy."

This was something that I had never thought about and quite honestly, I wasn't interested. My child had recently had surgery and had a feeding tube. My hands were full and although a part of me was searching for something more, I did not want to be bothered. I was in my own little world and wanted to be left alone.

However, this person was relentless and asked again. My feelings had not changed. I was not interested. Then, out of nowhere, an application to be a provider arrived in the mail. Shortly after that, a second application came.

At this point I was curious and a little annoyed. Why were these applications just appearing in my mail? Had my friend requested that these be sent to me? I talked to my husband and he suggested that I complete the application and see what happens.

By this time, I had misplaced both applications. That was my way out. However, to make sure I had covered my bases, I prayed, "Lord, if this is a direction You're leading me in, You and You alone are going to have to tell me and You are going to have to get me another application." Can you believe the next day I received an application? Although I had seen God's hand move in my life before, it never gets old and there is always a sense of amazement with it.

I completed the application and sent it in mid-March. They informed me it would take 60-90 days for the entire process. A week later I received an invitation for an interview. In less than 10 days I had my interview and by the end of April, I had a contract with the county. By May, I had my first consumer.

This was in 2005, the same year that Hurricane Katrina hit. On the day the storm began its destructive path, the floodgates opened. Just like the flood gates opened for Katrina, the flood gates opened for my business. At one point, I had 130 consumers in one day. I had only been a provider for 90 days. Statistically speaking, I should not have had that many consumers because I was the "new kid on the block." I didn't know anything about being in business or starting a business but there I was, providing a service for those that desperately needed it. It was exciting and a bit overwhelming.

Even in my delayed obedience, God opened the doors for me to walk in my purpose. We should never be delayed in our obedience. When God brings it to you, He's bringing it for a reason and a purpose. It's not for your purpose, it's for His purpose.

How to Know You Are In Your Purpose

I am often asked, "How do you know you are in your purpose?" For me the answer is simple. You know that you are in your purpose when you do what you do and it's effortless. This realization came to me as people would see me do what I do and comment on how it looked "effortless." That word stuck with me.

When you truly love what you do, it doesn't seem like work. The energy that you use doesn't feel like effort. You enjoy what you are doing. You are making a difference. That is what you are called to do.

I'm not called to be an accountant because I don't enjoy numbers. I don't enjoy organizing finances. Although I could do it, it would take effort for me to do. It would require a lot of effort on my part and it would take away from what God had put in me and called me to do.

I didn't know that I was gifted as a caregiver until I started caring for my child. It was a gift and talent that God blessed me with and it is something that I am passionate about.

What are you passionate about? What do you enjoy doing? What is the thing that comes to you that keeps you going? What is it that you enjoy doing that you do effortlessly? What things would you spend your time doing if money were not an issue? You will find your purpose in that area that lights you up, gives you joy, and brings glory to God.

When we identify those things that we are passionate about and use our gifts and talents that God has given us, we are giving God the glory.

Sometimes we are paralyzed by fear. We are afraid because we don't know what the outcome will be. We are afraid because we can't see how things will work out. There is a term that I use called "blind faith." But when you think about it, all faith is "blind faith." The definition of faith given in Hebrews 11:1 says:

Now faith is the substance of things hoped for, the evidence of things not seen.

The very nature of faith means that we do not see it, we are "blind." When we truly walk by faith, we can't see our next step. We don't know what is waiting for us around the corner or behind the door. We have to trust in God and know He has a plan for our lives. When we walk by blinded faith, we walk in the purpose that God has for our lives.

You're not going to be in your full purpose all at once. There is something called "purpose steps." It's one step at a time. If God sees you are faithful with a little, He can bless you with more. The more obedient you are, the more He can add to you.

When I started my business, God blessed me with one client, then two clients. I was faithful with them and then I had 12 to 15 clients over a three-month period. After that, the floodgates opened and blessings literally overtook me. God opened that door. I didn't know it and I didn't want it. It was not what I had asked for. However, when I became obedient and took action, even though it was delayed, He honored my obedience.

I repented for my slothfulness and I'm learning each day that when God brings me to it, there is something I need to do about it. I have to take action and stick with it. That's my purpose.

You may not see the entire picture clearly. As you walk daily in your purpose, the picture becomes clearer. God gives you the picture, the people, the places, and the pieces as you are walking

A delay in your purpose is not a denial of your purpose.
Sherry Donahue-Brown

in your purpose on your assignment. This is done in an effort to bring His vision to past.

To this day I cannot tell you where those applications came from. They just showed up at my house. I asked the person that approached me about the applications to see if they had them sent and they informed me that they had not. I don't know who God used to send those applications to me.

I hope you will reflect on the experiences in your life and on the things that were said to you that can possibly put you on the path of your purpose. What actions do you need to take today to begin walking in your purpose?

My Thoughts

What am I passionate about? What parts of my purpose have I identified so far?

My Biggest Takeaways and Action Items From This Chapter

Chapter 5 - Direction of Your Destiny

Direction – a course along which someone or something moves; the management or guidance of someone or something.

> ## Main Principle
> Write the vision and make it plain, so we can go from the Dream to the Direction to His DESTINY.
> #TheVoicelessChild

Writing the Vision

In the Bible, the Lord instructs us to write the vision and make it plain (Habakkuk 2:2). The practice of writing down inspirations, dreams, and visions has played a major role in my life and business. The idea for my business came to me in a vision. Although I had no idea what it meant, I wrote down what I felt the Lord was telling me. As I reflect back, I remember thinking, *Ok, what is this and where is it?*

When you hear from God, I encourage you to write it down. When you write it down, God will give you more. As God gives you more, He will also give you the vision. Don't overthink it. Just write down what you hear or feel. Don't try to figure it out. It may only be a couple of words. That's fine. Write those few words down. As you write the inspiration down and meditate on it, clarity will come and, as promised in the Bible, it will come to past. God may not give you the entire plan. Write down whatever it is that He gives you and then have faith that His Word is true. As Habakkuk 2:3 tells us, it may take a while, but it will come to past.

When I heard the name for my business, I wrote it down. A couple of days later, God gave me a little bit more. It was very early, about two or three o'clock in the morning. I woke up and began writing. Although I didn't know all of the details of my vision, I knew I would be helping people. I thought I would be a local helper.

When I finished writing what turned out to be three or four pages of information, I said, "Lord, what does this look like?" Later that evening, I saw the television show "Nanny 911." Nanny 911 was a realty show where families with hard-to-manage children would bring in a British nanny to help. Watching that show, I realized this is what my business would look like. I would be going to homes and helping families of children with behavior problems.

The vision was getting clearer. I remember praying, "Lord, if this be Your will, if this is what You are saying, then let me know by telling me what I need to do." God did just that. Shortly after that, I received a contract with a local adoption agency.

The agency asked for my pay expectations and I asked the Lord for the amount that I should ask for. I was a teacher and was accustomed to the pay being stated in the contract. God gave me a number and I wrote it down. I thought, *wow God, that's a big number!*

When I later met with the agency to discuss salary, I asked the question, "Where do you normally start?" The number that I had written down exactly matched their starting pay. I was amazed! When I left the meeting I immediately called my husband and said, "Baby, last night God gave me this number and I wrote it down and the number that I wrote down is what they are going to pay me per hour!"

My husband eagerly replied, "What number is it?"

I told him and he was blown away too. Although I trusted God and had complete faith in Him, I have to admit it was a little scary. That experience helped me to realize that God was not only directing my destiny, He was directing the steps of those around me towards my destiny.

My Vision Mindset

I had the dream. Now I needed direction. When I was a teacher, everything was laid out for me. But as a self-employed person, nothing was laid out for me. So God gave me some titles, catchy phrases, and other practical things to do for when I got out there. I quickly realized I needed God to give me an entrepreneurial mindset.

He did. I began to develop special behavior plans for my clients. As I implemented these plans for my clients, it began apparent that I was walking in my destiny. I began to use the gifts that God had so graciously bestowed upon me to start walking in my destiny.

My clients saw immediate results. They would often comment about how gifted I was in this area. When asked how I was able to affect the desire change in their homes, I would tell them it was a talent that came naturally to me. Since my contracts were often with government agencies, I could not talk about God in the family's home. But I knew in my heart that it was God. As you walk in the direction of your destiny, it seems effortless.

Dreams, Desires, and Direction

The dreams are the visions that God gave me. The desire to do what I was doing pulled me out of my comfort zone. I had to go into people's homes and I absolutely enjoyed it. The desire outweighed my discomfort. Your desire leads to your direction.

> *"Does your destiny determine your direction or does your direction determine your destiny?*
> Sherry Donahue-Brown

You begin with the dream, the desire that God places in your heart. The ideas that He inspires you with. All of these dreams and desires point to a destiny or a destination. But what lies between the dreams and the destiny is the direction. You may know where you want to go but the big question is, "How do I get there?"

Direction refers to the course along which something moves. It's the path from point A to point B. Oftentimes, you may not know the direction at the beginning of the journey. Unlike the GPS we talked about early, there is no button you can push to see the entire path that God plans to lead you to. It is often turn by turn. Very seldom does the direction come with a flashing neon sign saying, "Hey, this is the way to your destiny! Follow me!" Many times the direction will come from a quiet voice or from a casual encounter with someone.

For instance, I met a stranger and he asked me if I heard of a certain company, which I had not. He gave me the information and told me to call and speak to a certain person because they were always looking for good people. I reached out, completed the application, and was called in for an interview. It was that simple. When God gives you a dream and a desire, He gives the direction for you to go in.

Your Destiny

When you receive a word from God or a vision, write it down. Always keep a journal by your bed at night to write down the thoughts and inspirations you receive. Keep a small notebook with you during the day to record thoughts and ideas that you receive. Don't worry whether or not it makes sense; write it down anyway. You don't know how God is going to fit those pieces together or how He will direct you based on that information. I believe God gets each person to move strategically in a way that His will can be done in our lives. God is actually doing this in a way that He is truly going to get the glory. Write the vision; make it plain, so we can go from the Dream to the Direction to his DESTINY.

> *"We must absolutely commit ourselves to the Lord. Our direction, destiny, dream, and desire will all come from that commitment to Him."*
> *Sherry Donahue-Brown*

My Thoughts

What is my vision statement?

My Biggest Takeaways and Action Items From This Chapter

Chapter 6 - Obvious Obstacles or Overcoming Opportunities

Obstacle - something that obstructs or hinders progress.

> **Main Principle**
> You determine whether a situation will hinder your progress or advance you to success.
> #TheVoicelessChild

Obstacle or Opportunity

An obstacle is something that obstructs or hinders progress. How do we look at our lives—the trials and tribulations and everything we've endured? Many of us look at these as obstacles. I remember wondering why doesn't my mother love me? Why doesn't my father value me?

Do you see negative situations as obstacles or opportunities? We all have challenges in our lives. How you look at those challenges, whether you view them as obstacles or opportunities, will determine how you use them in your life. Will you allow the situation to hinder your progress or will you use the situation as a springboard to propel you closer to your destiny?

As I mentioned earlier, an obstacle is something that obstructs or hinders progress. On the other hand, an opportunity is a situation or a condition favorable for attainment of a goal; a good position, chance, or prospect as for advancement or success. Here is the key—you determine whether a situation will hinder your progress or advance you to success. The decision is yours.

When I think about the challenges in my life, I realize I initially saw them as obstacles and not opportunities. I looked at rejection as an obstacle, when I should have been looking at it as an opportunity. I looked at being homeless as an obstacle instead of an opportunity.

Whatever the obstacles are, we need to change our mindset and look for the opportunity for advancement and success. We need to ask ourselves the questions, "What can I learn from this experience? How can I use the knowledge that I am gaining from this experience to help someone else?" When you change your perspective, you will find the actual thing that is hurting you as an obstacle will make you stronger when you look for the opportunity.

> *"And be not conformed to this world: but be ye transformed by the renewing of your mind, that ye may prove what is that good, and acceptable, and perfect, will of God."*
> Romans 12:2

See the Opportunity

After a couple of years of prayer, God truly began to turn things around. He allowed me to love, trust, and He blessed me with a spouse. I am really thankful and grateful for my husband. I can truly say that God helped me to overcome that obvious obstacle. Because God blessed me, he gave me the opportunity to trust and love someone that He created and sent to me. Because of the challenges and experiences, I was able to see the true value of the opportunities that came to me.

There are many obvious obstacles that women face: rejection, disappointment, rape, molestation, poor self-esteem, and seeing themselves as not being good enough. These are obvious obstacles that hurt and cause us to put up hard walls and shells which don't allow people to enter our personal space.

> *"And we know that all things work together for good to them that love God, to them who are the called according to his purpose."*
> *Romans 8:28*

This also causes the inability to trust. I know that is how it was for me. But the Bible encourages us to be "transformed" or changed by the "renewing of our mind."

If we really, truly give all of that to God and allow God to actually renew our mind, renew our faith, renew everything in Him and through Him, God will take our disappointments and our discontentment and give us a direction for our destiny. We will truly be able to overcome those obvious obstacles and they will be obvious opportunities.

> *"The greater the obstacle, the more glory in overcoming it."*
> *Moliere*

My Thoughts

What is the biggest obstacle that I had had in my life that I can now turn into an opportunity?

_____

_____

_____

_____

_____

_____

_____

_____

_____

My Biggest Takeaways and Action Items From This Chapter

Chapter 7 - The Seven Keys to Discovering Your Purpose and Unlocking Your Destiny

Unlock - to lay open; disclose.

Main Principle
Everything you need for success is already in you.
#TheVoicelessChild

God has already given you everything that you need in life to be successful. It's in your DNA. In the Bible, the psalmist, David, made a bold statement in Psalm 139:14. It reads like this:

I praise you, for I am fearfully and wonderfully made. Wonderful are your works; my soul knows it very well.

Psalm 139:14 English Standard Version (ESV)

First, David praises God because he recognizes he was made in excellence. Now if you know anything about David's story, you know he had a lot of baggage. David struggled in his relationships with family, mentors, and friends. David struggled with his own selfish desires. So David didn't make this statement from a place of perfection.

Second, David recognized the works of God are wonderful. God is a master craftsman and He makes no mistakes. Each of us are made specially for the destiny that God has designed for us.

Finally, David acknowledges that he truly understands this. Our soul is the essence of us that includes our mental and emotional capacity. David truly understood that despite the struggles in his life, God made him and God made him to be something beautiful.

We have to truly understand the same thing. Regardless of your circumstances, regardless of your past or present struggles, God made you beautiful. Therefore, you have everything you need to be successful, to walk in your purpose and your destiny.

Let's unlock what it is we must understand in our minds to be able to walk in our purpose. Keys unlock things. They open things. They take us into opportunities, open doors, and reveal portals.

Key 1 - Awaken to the Possibilities

As we discussed in the chapter on Awakening, many of us are in an emotional state of sleep. We have shut ourselves down to the point that we are not aware of the things around us. It's similar to being physically sleep. When we are in a deep sleep, we are not aware of things going on around us. We are not aware of the people that may walk in the room. We are not aware of the conversation that is taking place in another part of the house. As a result, we don't engage with those people.

If someone walks into your room while you are sleeping, you are not going to have a conversation and engage with them while you are asleep, unless of course, you are talking in your sleep. In that case, you may say things, but you are just talking and probably will not even remember the conversation when you wake up. You definitely will not remember what the other person said to you. For the most part, you have a deaf ear to their conversation.

Sometimes we can have a deaf ear to God. We are not listening for His voice or sensitive to His leading. Many times we are not looking for God to speak to us. Therefore, when He does, we often miss it.

God can speak to us in many ways. He can speak to us through scripture or through the spoken word of a Pastor or teacher. He may speak to us through a quiet, still voice that we hear in our spirit. Sometimes He may speak to us through the actions that happen, such as an application showing up in our mailbox.

Even after we are sure that we have heard from God, we often feel that what we heard is too hard for us to accomplish. The truth is, it is too hard for us to accomplish by ourselves. That is why we need Him.

Wake up and hear what God is saying to you. Be open to the possibilities of what God has for you.

Key 2 - Be In Pursuit of Your Destiny

Once you are aware of the possibilities, you must decide to pursue your destiny. God has given you everything you need for the journey. However, you must decide that it is a journey that you are willing to take. He's given you the dream, the desire, the direction. You are now responsible to take the steps and make the effort to be successful in walking out your purpose and your destiny.

Being aware is not enough. For instance, just because you know that you would like to go back and finish school or pursue a different career doesn't mean that it will happen. You have to decide that you are going back to school. You have to decide that you are going to change careers. You must decide to move forward.

Although the applications showed up, if I did not decide to pursuit the opportunity, I would not have established my business. I had to make a decision. I had to decide that I would pursue it.

Oftentimes we get stuck at this point in the process because we don't see the entire picture. That's okay. Often God doesn't give us the entire blueprint. For me, I heard the name first. I didn't know what it meant. I didn't start out with a roadmap and a defined plan. I started by taking one action and then taking another action.

Key 3 - Take Action

> *"Remember, a real decision is measured by the fact that you've taken new action. If there's no action, you haven't truly decided."*
> Anthony Robbins

Now that you are aware of the possibilities and you have decided to pursue your destiny, it is time to take action. When God opens a door, walk through it. Walk through it with God's confidence, not in your confidence. When God leads you to it, He's going to bring you through it. He did not take you to it to leave you out there. This is where you truly have to trust God and not lean on your own understanding, as stated in Proverbs 3:5:

> *Trust in the LORD with all your heart, and do not lean on your own understanding.*
>
> *Proverbs 3:5 (ESV)*

Many times we get paralyzed when it comes to taking action because we are afraid of taking the wrong action. Don't allow a spirit of fear to stop you from moving forward. Make the call, submit the application, show up for the interview. Take action.

Key 4 - Define Your Circle

You know which direction you're going in. God has given you a dream. He's given you desire and He has given you a direction towards your destiny. Guess what? Some people can't go with you.

Think of a pyramid. The bottom part of a pyramid is very wide, but the higher you go up, the narrower it becomes. At the very top, it comes to a small point. That's how your circle becomes as you walk in the purpose in what God has for you.

This is often one of the most difficult parts of pursuing your destiny. You have finally figured out what it is that God wants you to do. You have made a decision to pursue your purpose. You start to walk in a new direction, taking action to fulfill the dreams that you have finally become aware of. But now you find that the people that were with you before you found this new direction are not as excited about this new journey as you are. It can be heartbreaking and disappointing. Unfortunately, it is necessary.

Not everyone is called to walk with us on our journey for the entire trip. Some people are only there for a few blocks. Others may be there for many miles and a select few are there for the entire course. That is okay. As we get to different segments in our lives, some people will fall off. We will also get new people in our circle as we begin attracting like-minded people. As we follow the direction that God has for our lives, He will always send people within our circle to help us and to support us.

Key 5 - Consistency

Now you are aware, you have made the decision to pursue your purpose, and you are taking the necessary actions, you must take those actions consistently. Consistency is the key to success.

"Success is the sum of small efforts, repeated day in and day out."
Maya Angelou

You can't make a decision to lose weight and diet for a day with the hope that you will reach your goal. You must be consistent. You must eat healthy on a consistent basis to see any real results. You must go to the gym regularly in order to achieve that goal. You can't have one healthy meal and one good workout today and then not have another one until next week. Each day you must take the actions necessary to achieve that goal.

It is the same with our destiny. You can't take inspired actions one day and then decide not to do anything for a month or a year. You need to consistently take the actions necessary to achieve your goal. Walking in your destiny is a continual process.

Key 6 - Perseverance

It is easy to be consistent when things are going well. However, when things begin to get rough, you must persevere.

There is no magic formula for perseverance. You have to just do it. You must work through the pain. You must work past the pain. Work through whatever you're going through. You must persevere with purpose

Many times, this is why our circle of influence must change. When things are rough, you need people in your ear telling you to keep going. You need cheerleaders in your corner shouting that you can make it. You need mentors that have accomplished big dreams to reassure you that you can do this. This is NOT the time for people to tell you that your dream is too big and maybe you should just forget it and go back to the way things were. This is the time that you must press forward.

Even if you don't have people in your corner, cheering you on, you must preserve anyway. Sometimes you may find yourself in the position of David, the beloved psalmist that we have referred to before in this chapter.

> *And David was greatly distressed; for the people spake of stoning him, because the soul of all the people was grieved, every man for his sons and for his daughters: but David encouraged himself in the LORD his God.*
>
> *1 Samuel 30:6*

David had to encourage himself. You have to become your biggest cheerleader. You must be your biggest fan and supporter. In pursuing your destiny, you may make decisions that will rub people the wrong way. In fact, let me assure you, you WILL make decisions that rub people the wrong way. That's okay. Find the strength to persevere. By the way, in case you are not familiar with David's story, he started out as a shepherd but ended up as a king.

Key 7 - Commitment

Finally, you must make a commitment. You must commit yourself to the Lord. I'm not talking about partially committed. You must make a decision to commit to what God gives you. Commit to the dream that He gives you and then watch Him open doors. Commitment is the key to being successful.

You must commit to become more aware of the voice of God in your life. **You must commit** to the decision that you have made to pursue your destiny. **You must commit** to taking action. **You must commit** to defining your circle and understanding that everyone is not in it for the long haul. **You must commit** to be consistent and persevering when things get tough. **You must commit** yourself to the Lord and to the purpose He has called you to.

> *"Commitment is the enemy of resistance, for it is the serious promise to press on, to get up, no matter how many times you are knocked down."*
> *David McNally*

I want to encourage you to use these seven keys to discovering your purpose and unlocking your destiny. If you need additional cheerleaders to encourage you and cheer you on, I want to personally invite you to our Facebook community, Destiny By Design Network, where we look forward to connecting with you and encouraging you to fulfill your dream. Come on over. We are waiting.

My Thoughts

Which of these 7 keys do I need to work on first?

My Biggest Takeaways and Action Items From This Chapter

Chapter 8 - Newness: Learning to Take Destiny Steps

Newness – something that is new; a new object; something of quality condition

> ## *Main Principle*
> You must pray, persevere, and pursue in order to reach your destiny.
> #TheVoicelessChild

When I think of something new, I think of purses and shoes. I think I have a love for purses and shoes because early in my adult life my purses were lost and I only had one purse.

I remember I broke the strap when my children were very young. It was raining and I was on my way to a doctor's appointment. I had a toddler and an infant along with a diaper bag and my purse. In the process of trying to carry everything, I broke the strap to my purse. I did not want, but needed, a new purse. I had no money at all to buy a purse. I was homeless and living in Salvation Army, waiting for the beginning of the month to receive my AFDC check (Welfare check). However, it was only the 19th or 20th of the month. While I was in Salvation Army, someone blessed me with vouchers for the Salvation Army Thrift Store.

I went to the Thrift store and found a purse. That purse was new to me because this was something I did not have but needed. Although I was grateful to be able to get the purse, I decided I didn't want to do this again. I didn't want to be forced to shop at the thrift store.

I remember praying, "Lord, I want to go to a mall and go to a real store and buy a purse." I will always remember that day. I felt that way with purses and with shoes. I said to myself, "One day, I'm going to be able to donate my purses here. I will be able to help someone else."

> *"It is better to live your own destiny imperfectly than to live an imitation of somebody else's life with perfection."*
> The Bhagavad Gita

In terms of newness, I think about the time I was homeless, living in Salvation Army and I had nothing. It was me and my two children, along with the two bags of clothes we owned. As I walked around, I had a carrier for the baby, a large black trash bag and my toddler had a backpack which held their snacks and the baby's bottles. I also had a baby bag and another bag. That was it.

During that four-month period between Christmas and Easter, God started to help me renew my mind while staying at the Salvation Army. Although I didn't recognize it as such at the time, God was actually taking me on a journey to newness through what I refer to now as Destiny Steps.

Destiny Step 1 – Prayer

I started praying like never before. I prayed, "Lord, I don't know what I'm praying for because I need everything." My needs were very great. I had an infant and a toddler and I was homeless. I had no way of getting my children what they needed and I was depending on the State for food stamps and AFDC check. My AFDC check was $128 per month. I had to figure out how to take care of my family with just that small amount.

At that point, I didn't really know what to pray for. I didn't want to be greedy in my prayer. I would just say, "Lord, help me. I don't know what to do. Lord, tell me what to do, because right now, I don't know and I'm overwhelmed."

Destiny Step 2 – Persevere

I had to persevere. I had no choice. Two beautiful babies where depending on me. It was truly hard because I needed to have a job. I needed interview skills. I needed everything. I had to accept whatever was going on. How was I to persevere when I didn't know how?

> "Hardship often prepares an ordinary person for an extraordinary destiny."
> C.S. Lewis

I had to just do it. Long before that became a slogan of Nike, it was a way of life for me. I had to just do it. I had to wake up every day and do what was needed. Each day I had to pray and ask God for strength.

Destiny Step 3 - Pursue

Not only did have I to persevere and not give up, I had to move forward. This was the most difficult because, quite frankly, I didn't know how to it. How could I pursue when I didn't know how to pursue? What was the purpose of me being homeless? How could I plan for what was to happen for my next step in life? This is what was on my mind while in the Salvation Army. I began to think and the persevering became harder.

A Mother's Nightmare

As a parent, the last thing you want is for your children to be sick. Most parents I know would do anything, including taking the sickness or illness on themselves, if possible, to avoid their child being sick. So it was devastating when my three-month-old infant had a stroke and almost died.

That feeling of helplessness when your child is sick can be overwhelming. Although the doctors assure me it was something that happens sometime and that it wasn't my fault, it was devastating.

Now, along with being homeless, I also had to deal with Child Services, another state agency. As I was there, praying and crying out to God, "I'm homeless. I have nothing and I'm about to lose my child. What else could go wrong in my life?" I was now facing eviction from the Salvation Army. My allotted time there was about to expire.

This is where perseverance comes in. At this point, all I had was God. I continued to pray and seek Him. I said, "Lord, how do you expect me to plan, prepare, and do anything if my time is up and my child is in the hospital? I have nowhere to go. I'm in a new state and I don't know anybody here."

You have to stay in the conversation with God. You have to continue to seek His wisdom, guidance, and comfort. I didn't even know what to pray for but I continued to pray. That's the point—you must pursue God, persevere, and continue to pray.

Here is what God did: God was able to extend my stay at the Salvation Army because my child stayed in the hospital for a while. Although I had to seek and gain employment, I lost that job because of my child's illness and his hospitalization.

With all of this going on, I continued to pray. I persevered through prayer. I could not see past the pressure and pain I was experiencing during that time. I did not have the ability to plan because the pain was so great. I could not figure out a purpose for what I was going through or how to get through at that time.

With the newness, God extended my stay at Salvation Army and He healed my child. As I was going through Child Services with the State, God blessed me to meet wonderful people that absolutely fell in love with my children. There was a requirement that I had to have a mentor with Child Services. I am still in contact with my mentor today. God turned it around.

> *"Everyone has their own destiny. Not everyone makes the choice to follow it."*
> The Lucky One.

We were able to move out of Salvation Army on April 1st. My child received in-home services because I did not have transportation.

Fast forward to today, my child that had the stroke has made wonderful progress because my prayer was for God to heal his body and make him whole. I am not unemployed but self-employed. I have become the employer and I provide jobs for other people. God has truly brought me a long way. I am walking in my destiny. To God be the glory.

My Thoughts

Which destiny step do I need the most help with?

My Biggest Takeaways and Action Items From This Chapter

Chapter 9 - Press Towards Your Purpose Through Your Pain

Press - to compress or squeeze; to embrace; to flatten or make smooth.

> ## Main Principle
> The purpose behind the pain is not to defeat you but to propel you towards your destiny.
> #TheVoicelessChild

When I think about pressing towards your purpose through your pain, I think about the scripture in Philippian 3:14. In the American Standard Version, it reads, "I press on toward the goal unto the prize of the high calling of God in Christ Jesus." In the King James version, it says, "I press toward the mark for the prize of the high calling of God in Christ Jesus."

When we're in pain, we don't want to press. When we're in pain, we don't want to be bothered. We want to be by ourselves.

According to the dictionary, press means to compress or squeeze; to embrace; to flatten or make smooth. So as I think about pressing through the pain in my life, I have to realize the purpose behind the pain. The purpose behind the pain is not for it to squeeze or to flatten me, but the purpose in the pain is to propel me towards the mark or the prize of the higher calling in Christ Jesus.

As long as I think about that, I know I will be powerful in my purpose. When I forget about my purpose and pressing, I know I am pitiful in my purpose. I can choose to be either pitiful or powerful, the choice is mine.

Root of Rejection

The most painful emotion we deal with is the root of rejection. The root of rejection either opens doors or closes doors. It lets you in or keeps you out.

> *"I can choose to be either pitiful or powerful, the choice is mine."*
> Sherry Donahue-Brown

Rejection is painful. I have dealt with the root of rejection through my mother. First, I was a foster child. I was taken away at the age of five. From my understanding as an adult, there was an opportunity for me to be returned, but I was not wanted. The state said either you take all of them back or none. We all stayed in the foster system until we were adults. I was rejected by my mother as a child, then rejected by my father as a young adult.

I went back to my birth mother in an attempt to have a relationship with her. I asked her questions about why she bought the other children birthday gifts and when it came to my birthday, she would say that she ran out of money. The same thing happened at Christmas where she would buy gifts for the other children but forget me. Why was I the forgotten one? What was wrong with me?

After an exchange of words, wanting to hear something, my mother told me, "I didn't want you, I never wanted you. I tried to kill you but you wouldn't die." I was a young adult, a single parent, and I was trying to make sense of my childhood. I was trying to avoid bringing negative emotions into my adult life. She said, "I tried to kill you, but you wouldn't die." My question was when. She told me it was when I was in the womb.

A Different Pattern

I had to press past that pain at that point because I was now a parent. I chose to pray and not to have the same pattern. The pattern that God gave me was different. God made me a different kind of parent for my children.

I prayed long and hard about this. I had always felt that my mother didn't want me but she now confirmed what I had felt for years. That was so painful. I asked God, "How can You give me parents where one tries to rape me and the other tries to kill me? She let me go and the state came and took me. Lord, what do you want me to do?"

> *"Rejection gives you more power to push forward."*
> Jeremy Limn

I had to press toward my purpose through the pain. At that moment, my purpose was being a single parent. My purpose was feeding my child and I needed a job. I went down the street to Taco Bell to work and I got a babysitter. I worked in the morning from 6am – 11am. It was not ideal but I realized this is what we had to do. Why? Because my purpose was being a parent.

After praying I realized my purpose and I had to walk in it. As a parent, I did not want my child to ever feel not being loved, accepted, and not being good enough. My purpose as a parent was to encourage, to discipline and, provide structure.

I was consistent. I was consistent in discipline. I was consistent in scheduling. We had breakfast, snack, lunch, and dinner.

Changing times were scheduled when I was working. Whoever was watching him had the schedule for feeding and changing.

As a child, I was not received or accepted by my parents. As a parent, my children were loved, accepted, encouraged, appreciated, and disciplined. I'm not saying that I am the best parent, but I worked hard to provide for my children what my parents didn't provide for me.

God blessed me to be a parent and I think that God gave me the ability to press and to turn my pain into the purpose of being a better parent for my children. I have been able to teach them the skills, abilities, and acceptance that they need to be successful, young, African American men in today's society. As we press to our purpose through our pain, it doesn't matter if you are not a parent, a single parent, or a grandparent. Stop inflicting the pain of our past onto our children. Change that pain into their purpose so they can become better people in their purpose that God has for their lives.

> *"Press towards your purpose through your pain."*
> Sherry Donahue-Brown

My Thoughts

What can I do to handle rejection better?

_____

_____

_____

_____

_____

_____

_____

_____

_____

_____

My Biggest Takeaways and Action Items From This Chapter

Chapter 10 - Can You Hear Me Now? I'm a Purpose Walker!

Walk - to pursue a course of action or way of life

> ## *Main Principle*
> Your true destiny is to walk in the purpose God has for you.
> #TheVoicelessChild

I have gone from a ward of the state, where I did not have a voice, to State assistance, to now being a state provider.

When I think about my journey, this scripture comes to mind: Philippians 3:15-16, "Let us therefore, as many as be perfect, be thus minded: and if in any thing ye be otherwise minded, God shall reveal even this unto you. Nevertheless, whereto we have already attained, let us walk by the same rule, let us mind the same thing."

I have pressed. I have been battered and I have been bruised. I have kept God first and He has revealed some wonderful things to me. God has already shown me things and allowed me to attain some of those things.

The scripture says, "Let us walk by the same rule, let us mind the same things." I think God is saying, "I am still here, I have not changed. If I have done it for you before, I will do it for you again." Not only is this powerful, it is comforting.

A Purpose Walker

I am now a purpose walker, walking in the purpose that God has for me. Everything I'm doing is what God has truly purposed me to do. For instance, my business is not something I chose to do or that I desired to do. It is something that God purposed me to do. I know now that we persevere with purpose.

When we are purpose walkers, we often find ourselves outside of our comfort zone. I am actually a shy person and I keep to myself. I don't talk about myself to others. Writing books, conducting workshops, and speaking on platforms around the country is not something I initially aspired to do. Expressing myself to strangers is not me. But I'm a purpose walker. I am walking into the purpose that God has for me. I'm not walking into what I wanted for myself, but for what God has for me

> *"I don't do things because I want to; I do the things God instructs me to do."*
> Sherry Donahue-Brown

The Results of Purpose

I remember when I was young, growing up in Louisiana. I was skinny. Kids would tease me and say I would never get a husband. I would always hear, "You will never do this or that." I can honestly say that today, I have been married for seventeen years and I'm just blessed by God with an awesome husband. I am so grateful for his kind spirit. He is very supportive. He willingly loves me through my hurts. I am forever grateful to God for preserving my husband and bringing him to me for such a time as this.

I have children. My baby that had a stroke is autistic and is doing wonderful. A few years back, one of their doctors suggested that I put them on a list to go into the state institution because they could not make a prediction on their condition or quality of life due to their rare disability. I did check out the list of other doctors, and I changed doctors.

When I changed doctors, I was interviewed and was asked, "What are you looking for?" I told them that I was looking for someone who was going to give me hope. I needed someone to give me hope in a hopeless situation. I was not naive and I understood the situation because I dealt with it every day. I just needed someone to give me hope. God blessed me with a doctor that does that for me and more.

Now, my baby is 22 years old and this is their last year in school. They are doing such an outstanding job. They have participated in Special Olympics and has won several gold medals. God has truly blessed me with a great family.

The victory didn't stop there. When I was homeless, I was riding the bus. I am no longer on the bus and God has blessed us with three vehicles. In my business we have four vans, making it a total of seven vehicles in our family. I am far from homeless. We now have two family homes and three houses for my business. God is good.

I went from being unemployed to now an employer of over 60 employees. We have become the largest minority owned agency in our county. I am the only African American person on the committee for providers in our state.

I am actively involved in church. I have almost completed the course, God's Leading Ladies. I have started a second business,

Persevere with Purpose, where I am a speaker and coach and I help other walk in their purpose.

In December 2015, God blessed me to have an event with the Salvation Army called Hope for the Holidays. I had a blanket and hat drive. God had me donate 75 blankets and 100 hats. With this being the first event, we had less than 30 days and in this time God blessed us to donate to the Salvation Army 83 blankets and 103 hats. This happened at Christmas time and it was so meaningful because years ago when I was homeless, I went to the Salvation Army at Christmas time and received a bed and blankets for me and my children.

> *"A purpose walker is always mindful of God's timing."*
> Sherry Donahue-Brown

When I think about my life and how I am, what I do and why I do what I do, I realize I do things because God instructs me to. I could have given back and donated years ago but God did not instruct me to do it then. God allowed it to happen in 2015. A purpose walker is always mindful of God's timing. If it is outside of His timing, then it is outside of His purpose and His will. Always be mindful of this.

I want to encourage you to walk in your purpose. You may feel voiceless, like I did in the beginning, but you must allow yourself to become awakened to your emotions and your own voice. You must find your direction or compass. Take the time to understand the your purpose and the direction of your destiny. Don't be discouraged by the obstacles. Learn how to overcome them and see the opportunities that they present. Work through the keys to discovering your purpose and unlocking your destiny.

> *"When you walk in purpose, you collide with destiny."*
> *Ralph Buchanan*

Appreciate the newness that is found in God and learn how to take destiny steps. Don't give up. Press towards your purpose through your pain. Let your voice be heard and declare, "I am a purpose walker."

You are not alone. Not only is God with you, but He has purposed that there are people like myself who have been called to help you walk in your purpose and unlock your destiny. If this resonates with you, I would love to connect with you. Join our Facebook community, Destiny By Design Network.

Remember, you are a purpose walker!

My Thoughts

What can I do today to show that I am walking in my purpose?

My Biggest Takeaways and Action Items From This Chapter

Main Principles

Although situations and circumstances can take your voice away and cause you to become silent and mute, it doesn't have to be permanent. Your voice can be heard.
#TheVoicelessChild

Just as your physical body needs rests so does your emotions and just as your physical body awakens, it's now time to awaken your emotions.
#TheVoicelessChild

We must follow the direction that God is leading us as we would follow a compass. If we have made bad choices, it's not too late to get back on track.
#TheVoicelessChild

When God has you on an assignment, He provides the picture, the people, the places, and the pieces in an effort to bring His vision to pass.
#TheVoicelessChild

Write the vision; make it plain, so we can go from the Dream to the Direction to his DESTINY.
#TheVoicelessChild

You determine whether a situation will hinder your progress or advance you to success.
#TheVoicelessChild

Everything you need for success is already in you.
#TheVoicelessChild

You must pray, preserve and pursue in order to reach your destiny.
#TheVoicelessChild

Your true destiny is to walk in the purpose God has for you.
#TheVoicelessChild

Quotes

"Without a voice, I'm invisible." - Sherry Donahue Brown

"Did vanishing words lead to the vanishing voice, or did the vanishing voice lead to the vanishing words?" - Sherry Donahue Brown

"Who can hear me? I need God to hear me." - Sherry Donahue Brown

"Emotions make you cry sometimes." - Sherry Donahue Brown

"It's time, it's time to make that change." - Sherry Donahue Brown

"Get up, Get up, Get your emotions up." - Sherry Donahue Brown

"The difference between what lies behind us and what lies ahead of us is the choice that we make in the moment." - Sherry Donahue-Brown

"The difference between the impossibility and possibility is your determination." - Sherry Donahue-Brown

"A delay is not a denial." - Unknown

A delay in your purpose is not a denial of your purpose. - Sherry Donahue-Brown

A delay in your purpose is not a denial of your purpose. - Sherry Donahue-Brown

"We must absolutely commit ourselves to the Lord. Our direction, destiny, dream and desire will all come from that commitment to Him." - Sherry Donahue-Brown

"And be not conformed to this world: but be ye transformed by the renewing of your mind, that ye may prove what is that good, and acceptable, and perfect, will of God." - Romans 12:2

"And we know that all things work together for good to them that love God, to them who are the called according to his purpose." - Romans 8:28

"The greater the obstacle, the more glory in overcoming it." - Moliere

"Remember, a real decision is measured by the fact that you've taken new action. If there's no action, you haven't truly decided."- Anthony Robbins

"Success is the sum of small efforts, repeated day in and day out." - Maya Angelou

"Commitment is the enemy of resistance, for it is the serious promise to press on, to get up, no matter how many times you are knocked down." - David McNally

"It is better to live your own destiny imperfectly than to live an imitation of somebody else's life with perfection." - The Bhagavad Gita

"Hardship often prepares an ordinary person for an extraordinary destiny." - C.S. Lewis

"Everyone has their own destiny. Not everyone makes the choice to follow it." - The Lucky One.

"I can choose to be either pitiful or powerful, the choice is mine." - Sherry Donahue-Brown

"Rejection gives you more power to push forward." - Jeremy Limn

"Press towards your purpose through your pain." - Sherry Donahue-Brown

"I don't do things because I want to, I do thing that God instructs me to do." - Sherry Donahue-Brown

"A purpose walker is always mindful of God's timing." - Sherry Donahue-Brown

"When you walk in purpose, you collide with destiny." - Ralph Buchanan

Made in the USA
San Bernardino, CA
06 July 2016